Original title:
The Whale's Breath

Copyright © 2025 Creative Arts Management OÜ
All rights reserved.

Author: Theodore Sinclair
ISBN HARDBACK: 978-1-80587-387-7
ISBN PAPERBACK: 978-1-80587-857-5

Chasing Shadows Beneath Waves

In the deep where shadows play,
Fish wear glasses, fish say "hey!"
A dolphin dances, quite the sight,
Tap dancing turtles join the fright.

Jellyfish drift, with style so grand,
While crabs are scheming, plotting a band.
Octopuses paint with colorful flair,
Throwing confetti in salty air.

Whispers from the Abyss

Bubbles giggle, secrets they share,
Anemones gossip without a care.
Starfish tell tales of their grand feats,
While squids scribble poems on seaweeds.

A turtle laughs, "I'm late, oh my!"
"Time's just a concept," the fish reply.
Seahorses duel, twirling with grace,
Creating a whirlpool in this vast space.

Inhale of a Blue Titan

A giant blimp called ocean's friend,
Breathes out bubbles that twist and bend.
Clownfish chuckle at the big blue,
"Can you even swim? Do you need a crew?"

With each giant puff, the waves do bounce,
Fishtails wiggle, all sea critters flounce.
"Careful with that, it's a slippery ride!"
As a wave rolls in, they all run and hide.

Breath of the Boundless Sea

In the aqua where laughter's found,
Seaweed dances, with moves profound.
Crabs share jokes, while dolphins squeal,
Currents swirl, they twirl and reel.

A splash of whimsy, tides of fun,
Octopuses juggle, one by one.
Gorgeous fins flash, in colors aglow,
Underneath the waves, a comedy show.

Shoreline Secrets of the Deep

On sandy shores we play and dig,
While fish nearby dance a funny jig.
The seaweed winks, a greenish grin,
As crabs hop sideways, with shells like kin.

A gull swoops down, it tries to tease,
Stealing snacks with the greatest of ease.
We laugh so hard, our bellies ache,
While sea stars giggle, for goodness' sake!

Rhythm of the Ocean Exhale

The tides roll in with a boisterous laugh,
Waves crashing down like a watery chaff.
With bubbles popping like fizzy drinks,
The fish below are plotting, I think!

They blow out bubbles that float and drift,
Turning the ocean into a gift.
While dolphins dance in swirling loops,
Their flips and flops are just silly loops!

Ocean's Heartbeat Beneath

Under the waves, there's a party tonight,
Mermaids giggle, all gleaming and bright.
They twirl with octopuses, oh what a scene,
With jellyfish gliding like balloons filled with cream.

The sea's a circus, a splashy affair,
With sea turtles wearing hats and flair.
They invite the whole ocean to join in the fun,
As laughter erupts like rays from the sun!

Mystique of the Submerged

Beneath the waves, there's a sound so bizarre,
Like a trumpet player who forgot where they are.
The fish all giggle, the shells start to sway,
As the orchestra bubbles, just playing away.

An old whale sneezes, a mighty big blow,
Sending sea cucumbers dancing in tow.
The corals chuckle, a colorful bunch,
While sea snakes wiggle, giving a lurch!

Breathe and Dream of Waves

In the deep where big fish play,
Air bubbles rise, then float away.
A creature laughs with mighty might,
Blowing puffs, what a sight!

Splashes dance and giggles roll,
In blue depths, they take their toll.
Gigantic friends in playful chase,
With a whoosh, they win the race!

Every breath's a giddy cheer,
Waves erupt, they draw us near.
A flip here, a twist up high,
Spray like confetti in the sky!

So take a breath and dive on in,
Join the fun, let laughter spin.
In the waves, we'll splash and glide,
With each gust, joy shall abide!

Song of the Vastness

Under the sun, big fins leap,
Songs echo through the ocean deep.
A chorus of giggles fills the blues,
As surfboards swap with gigantic shoes.

On the crest, the bubbles pop,
Like balloons that dance and drop.
Glistening tails flick in delight,
With each tune, the waves ignite.

Harmonies twist with ocean air,
Fins flapping like they just don't care.
A melody of splashes ring,
Who knew the sea could make them sing?

Oh, what mirth in salty spray,
With the vastness leading the way.
We'll laugh until the sun goes down,
In this frolic, there's none to frown!

Undercurrents of the Collected Souls

In shadowy depths, a congress thrives,
With giggles bubbling, joy dives.
Whimsical chatter fills the sea,
As tides of laughter flow with glee.

Beneath the surface, secrets hide,
In a swirling storm, they all collide.
Ticklish currents, a playful tease,
Bringing forth bubbles with effortless ease.

In this gathering of the jiggly-kind,
Each soul a potion, uniquely defined.
With beacons of laughter, they delight,
In the whimsical dance of day and night.

So join the party, don't be shy,
Wave your fins as you swim by.
In the ebb and flow, let's all partake,
Of this joyride that we make!

Whalesong of the Waves

The big ones munch while singing songs,
In the watery depths where joy belongs.
They hum a tune that's sure to please,
As the ocean sways and bends like trees.

With flips and flops, they make a splash,
Their playful tunes are quite the clash.
Bubbles rise, a delightful spree,
Their symphony flows, wild and free.

Each note carries waves of delight,
Making surfboards swirl, such a sight!
With every breath, they inflate the fun,
In this ocean party, everyone's spun!

So let's join in the joyous play,
As the giants glide in their own way.
Their laughter echoes through the blue,
Together we dance, me and you!

Undercurrent of Dreams

In the deep where bubbles float,
A fish in a tutu starts to gloat.
'The ocean's my stage,' it makes a scene,
While seaweed dancers twirl and preen.

A crab in glasses reads the news,
Sipping seawater, wearing blue shoes.
Fish giggle as they twist and flip,
As jellyfish don their best outfit.

Starfish gossip with their bright arms,
Telling tales of their underwater charms.
A dolphin cracks jokes, it's quite the show,
Making waves with laughter, don't you know?

In the depths where dreams collide,
Creatures frolic, with nothing to hide.
Bubbles burst like giggles in the air,
A carnival hidden, beyond compare!

Echoing Hues of the Sea

A octopus artist paints the floor,
With crayon coral and seaweed galore.
His canvas swirls in a magical way,
As fish applaud and clap in sway.

A porpoise surfer catches a wave,
With a flip and a splash, he's ever so brave.
Hilarious stunts, he flies in the white,
Making sea creatures laugh with delight.

Clams come out for a concert show,
Bopping their shells to the ocean's flow.
Turtles groove in rhythm divine,
While sea cucumbers sip on brine.

The sea's a stage, a wacky spree,
Filled with colors and laughs, oh so free.
As bubbles rise, the laughter grows,
With echoes of joy wherever it goes.

Song of the Silent Depths

Where silence reigns, and shadows play,
A whale sings tunes that make fish sway.
His melody's silly, all in good cheer,
With bubbles of laughter floating near.

Anemones waltz to the beat of the sound,
While crabs in a conga line dance around.
The currents twist, the laughter flows,
As everyone joins in, goodness knows!

Seahorses giggle, lost in the fun,
Playing hide and seek till the day is done.
Even the shyest of the finned say,
'I'm here for the song, come what may!'

So deep below, where the silence sleeps,
A chorus arises, joyfully leaps.
In quiet waves, the laughter's found,
As creatures unite, with happiness abound.

Rhythms of the Great Wide

In the vastness where treasures hide,
A clam DJ plays beats with pride.
His shells are spinning, the bass goes boom,
While the fish crowd around, filling the room.

A sturgeon twirls in a top hat grand,
Ballet in bubbles, upon the sand.
All sea life gathers for this delight,
As squids start to breakdance, what a sight!

Starfish snap selfies with their long arms,
Capturing moments of underwater charms.
With a flick of a fin, they pose with glee,
In the rhythms of life found beneath the sea.

As waves clap in time to the groovy show,
The ocean pulses with energy flow.
In laughter and dance, they find their stride,
Celebrating life in the great wide tide!

Symphony of Wind and Water

In the ocean's grand expanse,
Bubbles rise and fish rejoice,
The air is filled with silly sounds,
As sea creatures find their voice.

A splash and a puff, laughter flows,
With each playful, buoyant wave,
Tentacles tickle, fins take flight,
In the dance that the tides gave.

The seagulls squawk, the dolphins play,
A concert in the salty brine,
Where kelp sways and crabs tap-dance,
A watery stage where all align.

With every huff of ocean air,
A symphony of joy is born,
In this concert no one can miss,
Where the waves greet the break of dawn.

A Song of the Leviathan

In depths where sunlight seldom wriggles,
A giant sings a goofy tune,
With bass so low, it shakes the sea,
And bubbles rise like balloons.

His body sways with jolly grace,
As barnacles join in the fun,
Tickling each other in the current,
Chasing shadows, on the run.

With a whoosh and a splash, he twirls about,
Making waves like a merry-go-round,
All the fish clap with little fins,
As laughter echoes, profound.

A comic ballet in the blue,
With every flip, the ocean smiles,
In the realm of the unseen giants,
Where laughter floats for miles and miles.

Mysteries of the Deep Blue

Beneath the waves, a riddle swirls,
In the depths where the seaweed twirls,
A creature with a grin so wide,
Hides mysteries in its playful glide.

Its secrets spill like ocean spray,
As soft breezes dance and sway,
It tickles the sand with a cheeky laugh,
While fish scatter like tiny staff.

What swims below? Oh, take your guess,
A colossal joke, or ocean's jest?
With every splash, it winks and nods,
In the waters where whimsy prods.

The tales it tells, both weird and grand,
Leave us chuckling on the land,
For in every wave's delight,
Is the heart of the ocean, bright.

Rhythms of the Tidal Breath

Rhythmic sighs from below the waves,
Turn belly laughs, the ocean braves,
As tides roll in with squeaky charms,
They cradle fish in watery arms.

Each swell and dip, a playful jest,
The sea's heartbeat, it knows best,
A gurgling giggle, a tidal cheer,
Echoes through the ocean clear.

A narwhal nods with a toothy grin,
Joining in the watery spin,
With friends who frolic, twist, and jibe,
As salty breezes take their vibe.

The waves, they laugh, the currents hum,
With each chortle, the sea feels young,
In a grand ballet of soaking fun,
Where rhythm and laughter intertwine as one.

Breathless Reveries of the Ocean

A giant in the blue, how grand,
With flippers wide and views so bland.
He swims with grace, a submarine,
And makes the fish turn green with sheen.

He sneezes loud, like thunder's call,
The sea life ducks, they think he'll fall.
But who can blame a creature so vast?
It's hard to breathe when you swim so fast!

With bubbles flying, he's in the fray,
Sending little fishies on their way.
They giggle as they dart and dash,
While he just swims and makes a splash!

So let's all dance beneath the waves,
With laughter that the ocean saves.
For in these depths, we find delight,
In the hiccup of a whale, so bright!

Gentle Giants in Dreams

In the ocean's dream, they twirl and sway,
Gentle giants in a playful ballet.
With wiggly tails and giant grins,
They tease the fish and start their spins.

A tickle here, a bubble there,
Who knew they'd have such crafty flair?
They peek from below with a winking eye,
"Catch me if you can!" they seem to cry.

As they leap high, the dolphins cheer,
"Oh look at them, with little fear!"
They puff and blow, the ocean froths,
A comical sight that leaves us in troths.

With each deep breath, they let out a laugh,
Creating waves that dance in half.
For in their world, joy takes the lead,
Gentle giants, sure to succeed!

Guardians of the Tidal Twilight

When twilight falls, they start to play,
Guardians of dusk, making their way.
With heads held high and songs so grand,
They serenade the night so planned.

Their laughter echoes through the sea,
Bubbles rising, wild and free.
A shuffle and splash, the water gleams,
Like comedic actors in oceanic dreams.

They hoot and holler, what a scene,
With fins that flap and tails that preen.
As stars come out, they dance around,
In a tidal rhythm that knows no bound.

In this watery stage, they find their part,
Whale-sized chuckles flow from the heart.
A playful nudge, a splashy jest,
These guardians know how to have the best!

Ocean's Euphony of Breath

A symphony sung in bubbles and glee,
Each exhale a note from the deep, wild sea.
The ocean's Chorus, a whimsical crew,
With laughter that dances in melodies new.

They breathe out laughter, a whale's delight,
Creating waves like a musical rite.
The fish all giggle, as they swim near,
In a watery concert that all can hear.

A plop and a splash, the seagulls complain,
"Stop your antics, or we'll go insane!"
But the giants just chuckle, with no care to heed,
For joy in the ocean is all that they need.

From bubble to bubble, the fun never ends,
With each playful swirl, the ocean ascends.
A euphony here, where laughter is crowned,
In the depths of the sea, true joy is found!

Titan's Exhale

In the ocean's great expanse,
A titan hiccups, starts to dance.
Water leaps, and fish all flee,
"Please don't sit on me!" they plea.

With every puff, the waves do smile,
Splashing sailors all the while.
They laugh and joke, what a sight!
"Is it the fish or just the light?"

A bubble pops with a goofy sound,
As laughter echoes all around.
The sea's comedian takes a bow,
"Next show's at noon, don't miss it now!"

So when the blue begins to shake,
Hold onto dreams, no chance to break.
For in this jesting, deep-blue show,
The titan plays, putting on a flow.

Language of the Vast Blue

In the depths where the seaweed sways,
Creatures gossip in quirky ways.
A dolphin snickers, quite offended,
"Not another beach ball, that's just pretended!"

The octopus waves, "I'm not that shy,
Decorated arms, oh me, oh my!"
Together they laugh at all the blunders,
In a world of bubbles, and silly wonders.

"Did you hear that wave?" a fish would cry,
"It's telling tales of the seagull's pie!"
Echoes chuckle through currents wide,
As laughter bubbles, they can't hide.

So deep in blue, with giggles rife,
Under the waves, they live their life.
With each gurgle, they share a tease,
A language of fun carried by the sea breeze.

Depths Sing their Secrets

In the dark, where shadows creep,
The secrets hidden, oh they peep.
"Did you hear that?" whispers the eel,
"Our song of giggles, it's quite a deal!"

The jellyfish sway, with graceful flair,
"Careful now, don't stick a stare!
Our dance is bright, but don't you dare,
Touch my glow! I'm a superstar rare!"

Crabs in tuxedos strut with pride,
"Watch us waltz, don't run or hide!"
Clams chuckle, too shy to sing,
Beneath the waves, it's a funny thing.

As bubbles rise, they softly sway,
Secrets shared in their own way.
Through laughs and songs, the depths do sing,
In this underwater, joyous fling.

The Unearthed Ocean's Echo

From the deep, a sound arose,
A burble, a chuckle, and then a pose.
"What do you call a fish with no eyes?"
The sea floor giggles, "I'm not that wise!"

The sandbank waves, "I've seen it all,
From fancy ships to beach ball brawl."
Anemones laugh as they sway in time,
With the echo of waves, in rhythm and rhyme.

The coral reefs join, a colorful cheer,
"Join us for jokes, our time is near!"
As krill and plankton giggle too,
In the ocean's echo, a humorous crew.

So when you dive beneath the blue,
Hear the laughter, it's calling you.
For under the waves, where spirits flow,
Lies a funny world, an ocean show.

Breath of the Infinite Blue

In the ocean's deep blue flair,
A giant sneezes, what a scare!
Fish fly by, a sight to see,
Who knew they'd swim with such glee?

Bubbles rise like tiny stars,
Frogs with fins and dancing marbles.
A dance party under the waves,
Where jellyfish misbehave!

With each puff, the sea does laugh,
Mermaids swim, they love to gaff.
A tickle in the salty air,
Giant giggles everywhere!

So, here's to the blowers so grand,
Creating chaos in their band.
What's grander than a whale's grand snort?
Join the fun, with laughter as sport!

Guardians of the Mist

Beneath a shroud of silvery gray,
Guardians frolic, come out to play.
With a spout here and a splash there,
They keep the ocean light as air!

Flipping fins and friendly grins,
They tease the dolphins, the game begins.
"Catch me if you can!" they call,
As seagulls laugh and crabs stand tall.

Mysterious shadows glide and swirl,
Tickling the sea's playful curl.
At every puff, a wave of cheer,
These guardians spread joy far and near!

With their laughter, the sea rejoices,
Every splash, in perfect choices.
In misty echoes, tales are spun,
As they play 'til the day is done!

Ocean's Whisper

In the turquoise depths where secrets float,
A whale whispers with a giddy note.
"Listen close, I have a tale,
Of bubbles popping, and jellyfish fail!"

With wiggles and wobbles, they tell the scene,
Of seaweed parties and kraken's cuisine.
A beluga's giggle, a puff of surprise,
Where laughter dances 'neath sunny skies.

The clownfish chuckle as they glide,
A wave of mirth they can't abide.
"Come join us!" they bubble with delight,
While sea cucumbers sleep through the night.

Every expanse is filled with joy,
As creatures play with every ploy.
In the ocean's whisper, fun swirls so vast,
Let's float along on this current of blast!

Power of Submerged Giants

Under the waves where shadows roam,
The giants gather, far from home.
With playful dives, they show their might,
Creating tidal waves of pure delight!

Watch out, fish! The fun begins,
With splashes, giggles, and cheeky grins.
A sea turtle's shell gets a bath,
In joyful chaos, they draw their path.

Each powerful push sends bubbles high,
As sea stars twinkle in the sky.
"Bet you can't catch us!" they tease with glee,
Oh, the mischief of the deep blue sea!

So here's to the giants, both big and grand,
Who make the ocean a whimsical land.
With every laugh and playful jest,
They remind us all that life's a fest!

Bubbles and Murmurs

In the ocean's dance, they play,
Puffing bubbles, bright and gay.
Swirling laughter all around,
Giggling fish, and joy unbound.

With a splash and a little swirl,
They invite the sea to twirl.
Under waves, the antics flow,
Chasing tails in a grand show.

A flippered friend does a flip,
Gulping down a fun-filled sip.
Bubbles pop with silly sounds,
As lines of joy form merry bounds.

In this blue, where glee abounds,
Sea creatures spin with silly rounds.
With every breath, the fun expands,
Echoes of laughter, where life stands.

Ghostly Breaths in the Abyss

In darkened depths, a legend stirs,
A gentle giant, filled with purrs.
It sneezes once, the sea does quake,
And friends all giggle at the wake.

With misty breaths that swirl and fade,
They weave a tale, a ghost parade.
A mighty puff, the bubbles fly,
Scaring fish with a soft sigh.

Deep down below, where shadows gleam,
Nautical jokes become the theme.
With every gurgle, laughter's near,
They toast with water, full of cheer.

A trickster in the moonlit deep,
Where laughter dances, and secrets keep.
In haunting fun, they play their game,
A splash of joy, the ocean's fame.

The Ocean's Soliloquy

In a tide that sways and swirls,
The sea sings songs of playful girls.
With splashes and laughs in perfect tune,
Beneath the sun and the cheeky moon.

Each wave whispers tales of cheer,
Of fish and friends that gather near.
With watery giggles, the surface breaks,
A chorus of life, that's what it makes.

As salty winds tickle the shore,
Creatures gather for one encore.
With every breath and every tease,
The sea enchants with effortless ease.

In this ballad of bubbles and glee,
The ocean muses reflectively.
A symphony of joyous sighs,
Where laughter lingers and never dies.

Depths Stringing Their Chords

Beneath the waves, a melody grows,
A giant hum, that's how it goes.
With every wheeze and friendly puff,
The laughter spreads, never enough.

A chorus of splashes, a concert grand,
Fish tap-dance to the ocean's band.
With each deep note, hearts spring high,
As bubbles burst and seahorses fly.

In the deep blue, where the music flows,
Sea creatures gather, in sparkly clothes.
They strum the currents, a jolly tune,
While singing softly to the moon.

With whimsical rhythms, they sway,
In perfect harmony, they play.
In watery depths, their joy is clear,
Where laughter sounds, and smiles steer.

Kisses from the Coastal Abyss

Splashing waves in a silly ballet,
Fins flapping wildly, come join the fray.
Underwater winks and fishy grins,
Giggles bubble up with each wave's spin.

Jellyfish float like balloons in the blue,
Trying to dance, but they just goo too!
A sea cucumber's slow-motion glide,
Invites little fish for a ride full of pride.

Clownfish chuckle in a vibrant maze,
Telling tall tales of their underwater days.
Bubbles burst like jokes in the salty air,
As seaweeds sway without a single care.

Amidst the kelp, a party we'll host,
With all our friends, let's dance and boast!
The ocean's laughter, a symphony bright,
Kisses from the depths, a joyous delight.

Dancing with Ocean Shadows

In the dim of twilight, shadows prance,
Octopus tango in a curious dance.
They twirl and spin with shimmering arms,
Hiding shyly behind coral charms.

A starfish stumbles, trips on a shell,
Laughing so hard, it might just fell.
Setting the stage with a curtain of foam,
Critters gather, this ocean's their home.

The moon dips low, a spotlight aglow,
While sea horses hustle, putting on a show.
Crabs click-clack in time with the beat,
Choreographing fun, oh what a treat!

Flipping and flopping, with glee in the tide,
Anemones cheer on from the side.
Together they dance, under sapphire skies,
In the world below, laughter never dies.

Murmurs of Forgotten Giants

Whispers of titans echo so loud,
As seashells gossip, drawing a crowd.
The currents chuckle, old tales to weave,
While sea stars wink like they've just deceived.

A blue whale's giggle shakes the deep,
Rattling fish as they try not to peep.
Surfers surf on the backs of shrimp,
While dolphins wink with a playful skimp.

Mysteries churn, in bubbles they speak,
Crabs with their claws click when they seek.
What's past is present, so join in the fun,
With jests and jigs until the day's done.

Tales spin like whirlpools, around and around,
In this watery world, laughter is found.
Forgotten giants, with hearts filled with cheer,
Murmur sweet nothings for all to hear.

Fluttering Through the Sea Mist

In the morning mist, sea turtles race,
With flippers waving like they're in space.
Jellyfish float, like balloons set free,
Wobbling and bobbing, what a sight to see!

Puffers puff up with the silliest glee,
Making faces like they just want to be.
Gulls caw and call, as they swoop and dive,
Creating a ruckus, in the ocean thrive.

The salty breeze carries laughter anew,
As schools of fish form a shimmering crew.
Dancing in circles, they swirl and spin,
Tickling the bubbles, where fun will begin.

Even the seaweed joins in the game,
Swaying and laughing, it's never the same.
As the sun rises, the waters ignite,
Fluttering with joy, what a marvelous sight!

Whispered Legends of the Sea

In the depths, giggles swirl,
Fins like flags, they dance and twirl.
Echoes of a playful splash,
As bubbles rise, they spin and crash.

Tales of monsters in disguise,
Flipping fish beneath the skies.
With a fluke, they reach the shore,
Make you laugh, you'll ache for more.

Giant tails that wave hello,
In a splash, they steal the show.
Fishy friends with silly grins,
They play tag with salty fins.

So when you hear the ocean's cheer,
Know that laughter's always near.
For legends live in waves so free,
Where giggles flirt with mystery.

Lurking Giants' Lullaby

Hush now, hear the lullaby,
Monsters lounging, oh my, oh my!
Giant grins and playful winks,
In the dark, they laugh and clink.

With a blow, they send a spray,
Chasing clouds, they joke and play.
Their shadows loom with silly grace,
In the deep, it's a pillowcase!

A creature yawns, the surface shimmers,
Underneath, the humor glimmers.
Sideways glances, keels a-rock,
Lurking giants, jesters in the dock!

Slumbering now, they dream and snore,
Making waves that shake the shore.
A joyful ruckus, so profound,
In this depth where fun is found.

Serenading the Salty Depths

Bubbles burst in rhythmic beats,
A symphony beneath the fleets.
Gurgling laughter from the blue,
Every splash a joyful cue.

Dolphins join in on the fun,
Cartwheeling 'neath the warming sun.
With a wink and playful dart,
They serenade the ocean's heart.

Tales of treasure, fish that wear
Pirate hats and laugh with flair.
Every wave a chuckling sound,
In this dance, pure joy is found.

So raise a glass of salty brine,
Join the chorus, feel the shine.
As the depths croon a radiant tune,
Your spirit lifts, like a balloon!

Breaches of the Infinite Blue

Once upon a wave, they leap,
In the blue, then under, deep.
With a splash, they steal a kiss,
Navigating bubbles of bliss.

Tails that twirl, a joyful sight,
Under the moon, they dance at night.
Every breach's a laugh so loud,
Making shells form a cheering crowd.

In the depths, they plan their pranks,
Building castles, forming ranks.
Giant fish with silly hats,
Plotting jokes and chubby chats.

So when you glimpse the gleeful sprays,
Know they're jesting in their plays.
Breaches rise to greet the skies,
Full of laughter, and no goodbyes!

Symphony of Leviathans

In oceans deep, with glee, they play,
Blowing bubbles that drift away.
A splash, a giggle, a hefty thump,
Dance with fish, oh what a jump!

Underwater trumpets, a frothy sound,
Creating melodies all around.
With every puff, they stir the tides,
While seagulls laugh and take their sides.

They twist and twirl, a wobbly dance,
Flipping seals who seize a chance.
"Did you hear that?" whispers a fish,
"Sounds like a drumming, oh what a swish!"

So dive on in, join the fun,
With leviathans, laughter's never done.
In rippling waves, we'll wave and sing,
Celebrate joy, for life's a fling.

Echoes from the Abyss

Beneath the waves, a loud guffaw,
Echoes of laughter, what a jaw!
With every blowhole, a joke takes flight,
Whales cracking wise, oh what a sight!

"Why did the fish refuse to play?"
Because the whale made too much spray!
Well, they chuckle and jive as they glide,
Creating ripples, a giggly tide.

A chat with a crab, who's on their case,
"Can't catch a wave with that funny face!"
The mollusks chuckle, it's quite a spree,
In the underwater comedy, joy runs free.

So dive below, let laughter ring,
Where marine friends know how to swing.
Giggles and splashes, tales they weave,
In the depths of blue, who wouldn't believe?

Gentle Giants of the Sea

Gentle giants, rolling through,
Making waves with each old woo-hoo!
With a flip and a swish, they tease the tide,
Wiggly tails and giggles inside.

"What's that noise?" a dolphin will say,
"Just a whale cracking jokes, hip-hip-hooray!"
From spouts of water, they send a spray,
As fish all gather to see the play.

Flip-flopping friends in the salty mist,
With wiggling fins, they can't resist.
Laughing loud at a dolphin's dive,
This underwater crew, so fun, alive!

So come aboard, join their grand scheme,
Where mirth flows freely, it's quite a dream.
Amongst the bubbles and cheerful sound,
In the ocean's heart, joy is found.

Song of the Saltwater Mist

In the salty air, where giggles waft,
The sea's big tune, a lively draft.
With plumes so high, they puff and play,
Creating joy in the sun's warm ray.

"Can you hear that?" a little fish asks,
"It's whales in chorus, no need for masks!"
Harmonies bubble, splashes abound,
In this ocean concert, laughter is found.

They flip and flounder, sing silly rhymes,
Timing their tunes like perfect chimes.
With every note, the tide swings wide,
Creating a ruckus, where joys collide.

So join the revelry, dive right in,
Where shimmery scales are sure to win.
In the saltwater mist, so light and free,
We sing along with the jubilee!

The Breath Beneath the Surface

In the ocean's gentle sway,
A secret giggle floats away.
Bubbles rise like silly thoughts,
Beneath the waves, all wisdom's caught.

Fish wear hats, they dance and play,
With each puff, they joke all day.
Who knew the sea was such a clown?
And soft waves never wear a frown?

The water's pulse is filled with cheer,
Blowing kisses far and near.
The light shines bright, the fun won't cease,
With every gulp, there's pure release.

So whack your fins, and take a dive,
In this blue world, you'll feel alive.
For laughter bubbles all around,
In this vast playground, joy is found.

Waking to Ocean Reveries

Woken by a splash so grand,
I giggle at the sea's command.
A silver fin, a leaping joke,
In morning mist, the laughter's woke.

As dolphins dance like kids at play,
They blow up bubbles, bright and gay.
Who knew they were such skilled jesters?
Splashing humor like true testers!

The sun peeks in with a grin so wide,
Join the waves, it's a joyful ride!
Seagulls swoop with silly cries,
Making the best of sunny skies.

Embrace the whimsy of the blue,
Where jokes and giggles come in two.
The ocean whispers with a chuckle,
In its embrace, we all can snuggle.

Immense Pulse of the Blue

Behold the swell, a mighty joke,
A rumble, a giggle, the ocean spoke.
With every breath, a ripple flows,
Puffing clouds where laughter grows.

Creatures whirl in a vibrant game,
Hiding their giggles, but not their fame.
Mermans grinning with coral charms,
In their realm, there's no need for alarms.

The waves take turns, they crash and slap,
Causing fish to dance and clap.
Each pulse a sonnet, a joyous wail,
Deep undersea, they tell a tale.

So dive deep where the fun won't stop,
In bubbles and splashes, we twist and hop.
With nature's humor, the sea ignites,
In this buoyant world, we find delights.

Secrets from the Deep

Down where the sunlight barely peeks,
Live the jokesters with silly streaks.
Octopuses hold their breath in laughs,
Tickling each other in goofy halves.

Anemones tease with a wave and a sway,
While turtles chuckle and glide away.
A crab takes a bow, with pincers aflare,
Creating laughter, without a care.

The whispers of currents bring tales unspoken,
Of frolicking fish, and hearts unbroken.
In the dark, where mischief waits,
The ocean's humor simply dictates.

So float along and enjoy the ride,
In the depths where secrets cannot hide.
For every splash, there's joyous fleet,
A cheeky world beneath our feet.

Nautical Serenade

A giant glider, grinning wide,
Blowing bubbles, what a ride!
With a splash and a thud, oh what a sight,
Fish giggle and dance with delight.

He flips and flops, a clumsy show,
With a tail that sends waves in tow.
Stars above blink in the night,
As sea life joins the ribald fright.

Hear the giggles in the tide,
As krill and crustaceans all confide,
That this big fella takes the cake,
With every breath, the ocean shakes.

So here's to our blubbery friend so gay,
Making mischief in ocean's spray.
Let's toast to laughter, to glee so pure,
In the salty blue, joy will endure!

Flow of the Abyssal Air

In the deep, where the shadows loom,
A hefty prince stirs up the gloom.
With a puffy puff and a huffing sigh,
He sends sea cucumbers swirling by.

Gaily he swims through bubbles bright,
Creating whirlpools of pure delight.
With each exhale, a gassy plume,
He puts the clowns in the ocean's room.

As dolphins laugh and seaweed sways,
Our hefty pal steals the day's displays.
With a rollicking roar from his blubbery throat,
He turns mere bubbles into a boat!

So here's to the air, and the giggly fun,
From dusk till dawn, life just begun.
With every flow, a land of cheer,
In the depths of the sea, our hearts hold dear!

Breathless Dance in the Blue

Beneath the waves, a party starts,
A giant jester with oceanic smarts.
With a whirl and a twirl, he brings the fun,
Leaving fish rolling, oh, what a run!

His breath a melody, a bubbly tune,
Even the starfish clap in full moon.
With each silly leap, he prances around,
Creating a circus from sea to ground.

And the sea anemones sway in time,
To the rhythmic beats, so sublime.
"Join me!" he cries with a comical puff,
His dance, they agree, is just the right stuff!

So let's celebrate, let's give a cheer,
To our buoyant mate, let's draw him near!
With breath and laughter, we frolic too,
In this swirling, twirling oceanic view!

Reverie of the Ocean

Where the water whispers and giggles loud,
Dwells a dancer, of whom we're proud.
With a giddy gurgle, he lounges with flair,
Filling the sea with his breath of air.

He puffs like a balloon, oh what a scene!
Turning the ocean into a sparkling sheen.
Fish flip and flounder, all in a whirl,
As bubbles erupt in a jovial swirl.

Each plop and splash ignites hearty glee,
In this underwater jubilee!
With waves of laughter that never cease,
Our jolly giant brings us peace.

So gather 'round and sing along,
To the tune of the deep, to the sea's own song.
With mirth and mirages, we dance 'neath the sky,
In this reverie where we all can fly!

Exhalation of the Ocean's Heart

Rolling big and round, quite a sight,
Blowing bubbles with all their might.
Splashing laughter in the salty breeze,
Tickling fish, oh, what a tease!

With a puff and a blow, they make waves,
Podded jokers in watery caves.
Playing tag with the clouds up high,
Winking at seagulls as they fly.

Each breath a splash, a comedic roar,
Filling the ocean, asking for more.
Seaweed sways with a giggling cheer,
"Who blew that? It was not me, dear!"

In watery dance, they twirl and leap,
Making us laugh, their secrets to keep.
Under the sun, their fun doesn't cease,
Bubbles and laughter, a crustacean feast!

Lullabies of the Great Depths

Down below where the darkness hums,
Gentle giants sing out funny drums.
Their lullabies echo, a silly tune,
Making fish giggle beneath the moon.

A gentle croon, like rocks in love,
Surprising dolphins, swooping above.
"Was that a burp?" a seagull cries,
As laughter bubbles in sparkling sighs.

With every note, a tickle take flight,
While starfish dance with sheer delight.
A symphony filled with giggle and cheer,
Telling silly tales of the ocean near.

In watery slumber, the creatures dream,
Of humorous antics and friendly steam.
While waves dance softly to their call,
Great depths hold secrets, and laughter for all!

Giants Underneath the Surface

Beneath the waves, giants do lurk,
With sly grins hidden, oh what a perk!
Tickling turtles with their big tails,
Spinning around like lively gales.

Gigantic giggles escape from below,
"Who's the biggest? Let your sizes show!"
Shouting measurements 'til the seas shake,
A contest of faces, what a fun take!

"Look at my blubber!" one proudly boasts,
While others float like underwater ghosts.
Belly-flops echo, causing a splash,
Beneath the waves, they all have the bash.

In this ocean party, there's never a frown,
As they pratfall and swim in their underwater town.
With a wink and a wave, they dance in delight,
These underwater giants, pure laughter in flight!

The Pulse of the Sea Monster

Hear the rhythm, a pulse so grand,
The ocean chuckles, oh isn't it bland?
With each heartbeat, the waves come to play,
As the monster grins, ready for sway.

Flipping and flopping with scales that shine,
Making fish laugh, what a good time!
Tickling the reefs with playful intent,
As they cruise along, joyfully bent.

Every thump a wave, every roll a cheer,
The sea monster's heartbeat fills us with beer!
Swirling in circles, their fun never ends,
Why not join in? Say "hello" to friends!

A dance of bubbles, a waltz of the sea,
With the pulse of laughter, wild and free.
Tales of mischief, under the moon's glow,
As we bob alongside, laughing in tow!

Forgotten Melodies of the Waters

In a realm where fish sing,
Tuning forks made of shells,
Notes bubble up with a bling,
While octopuses play bells.

Pufferfish dance in a round,
Waving fins, oh what a scene!
Each blow a comical sound,
As they puff up like a bean!

The turtles join in the fun,
Tapping toes on coral floors,
Their laughter just can't be undone,
As jellyfish open doors.

A school of guppies takes flight,
With goggles made of seaweed,
Blasting tunes deep in the night,
A concert for all, guaranteed!

Guardians of the Liquid Kingdom

Beneath waves, where laughter roams,
Fish patrol with silly hats,
They wave to crabs in sandy homes,
While seahorses do acrobats.

A stingray glides, all smooth and cool,
Winks and honks, quite the sight!
Those dolphins, oh, they rule the school,
With flips and tricks, pure delight!

The clownfish splash, strutting about,
Jokes in every bubble burst,
Making sure there's never doubt,
That laughter's always quenched first.

In this realm beneath the blue,
The guardians keep fun at heart,
With every wave, a joyful cue,
Reminding us we're all a part!

Beneath Tides

In the depths of ocean's sway,
Lurks a thing with such a grin,
Dancing fish in disarray,
As laughter bubbles from within.

Octopuses run a race,
Ink jets shooting in the calm,
While sea turtles set the pace,
To the seaweed's catchy psalm.

Bright sunbeams play hide and seek,
Casting shadows on the ground,
Creatures chuckle, so to speak,
As a giggle softly sounds.

Under waves, the fun's not shy,
Play all day, from dusk till dawn,
In the blue, where spirits fly,
A laugh, a squirt, until we're gone!

Giants Dwell

In the deep, where giants dwell,
They swim with whims and jolly glee,
Singing songs, oh what a swell,
Echoes ripple, wild and free.

A whale with glasses, wise and old,
Tells fishy tales with a flair,
Of treasure hunts and gems of gold,
While sea cows munch without a care.

Here's a shark who can't help but smile,
As crustaceans tease his teeth,
He grins, and swims another mile,
In a world of laughter beneath.

Amidst these giants, joy persists,
Water dances, laughter flows,
With every tale and every twist,
The ocean's secret fun just grows!

Breath of the Celestial Ocean

Up above, a splash of stars,
Down below, the sea's sweet breath,
Celestial dances, within jars,
As laughter whispers of life's depth.

An astronaut fish tries to float,
In a bubble made of dreams,
Sailing 'round on a sassy boat,
Riding waves of cosmic beams.

The crabs all wear their finest gear,
For an intergalactic show,
With twinkling lights, they're full of cheer,
As sea stars shimmy to and fro.

In this watery universe, bold,
Where joy and laughter intertwine,
The push and pull of stories told,
Leave smiles afloat, forever shine!

Fluid Verses of the Deep

Beneath the waves, where fish do play,
A giant sneezes, clear the bay!
With bubbles popping, what a sight,
He waves his tail, oh what a fright!

He swims and grins, his blubbery jig,
Wobbling around, doing a big gig.
While dolphins laugh, they swim in a line,
Saying, "Look at him dance, isn't it fine?"

Waves splashing high, oh dear, oh me!
He opened wide, lost a fish, you see?
Now that one's hiding, no time to munch,
He glides on by, in a goofy bunch!

With sonar jokes, he makes quite a ruckus,
Telling tall tales, which cause much fuss.
Just another day, in his watery spree,
Life under the waves, so silly and free!

Echoes of the Deep

In the depths, a snort, oh what a sound!
It echoes back, making waves all around.
Fish scatter quick, darting from the blast,
While our big friend giggles, having a blast!

He puffs out a cloud that dances and swirls,
Tickling the seaweed, giving it twirls.
With a belly full of sea-soaked fun,
He spits out water, like a rare old gun!

The crabs do a jig, the octopus too,
They laugh at the bubbles, so shiny and blue.
"Goodness gracious!" they all squeal with glee,
As the gentle giant flexes, "Come swim with me!"

An orchestra plays, from depths wide and deep,
A symphony of laughter, no time for sleep.
With every wave, countless chuckles arise,
As our playful giant dances, a whale-sized surprise!

Currents of the Colossal

A mighty beast, with a wink and a grin,
He sways to the music, let the fun begin!
With a gargantuan leap, he splashes about,
Making waves of laughter, without a doubt.

The clams drop their pearls, in shock and delight,
As he flips through the sea like it's all so light.
Mollusks start clapping, in their shellfish way,
Cheering him on, in a watery ballet!

Barnacles bobbing, in rhythm and cheer,
Swaying along, as he draws them near.
"Join my merry crew!" he calls to the fish,
"For today we're a part of a great big wish!"

With a whirl and a swirl, he takes to the skies,
A leap through the air, oh what a surprise!
Down through the blue, in a thunderous splash,
In the currents of giggles, they all make a dash!

Serenade of the Ocean Giant

Under the sun, with a wink of his eye,
He sings to the schools as they flutter on by.
His voice like a song, echoes through the tide,
Creating joy, like a merry ride!

With flukes aloft, he dances and spins,
The little fish cheer, as the shenanigans begin.
He twirls in the water, all frothy and grand,
A generously large party, a finned wonderland!

Upside-down he glides, such a curious show,
As seagulls cackle, all gathered below.
"Who needs a stage, when you've got the sea?"
He chuckles along, as carefree as can be!

With bubbles as confetti, they join in the song,
A whimsical gathering, where all can belong.
Life's a little silly, when you're big and you're bold,
In this grand serenade, pure joy unfolds!

Echoing Calls of the Abyss

Down in the deep, where the bubbles float,
A fish wears a hat, and he sings in a boat.
With each echoing call, they dance in a line,
Doing jiggy little moves, feeling mighty fine.

Puffing out air like a dragon in flight,
Squid with a trumpet, oh what a sight!
Sea turtles clap, while the clownfish just grin,
As the orchestra plays with a splash and a spin.

Jellyfish sway in a wobbly groove,
A mermaid appears, with a shimmy and swoon.
In the deep dark blue, they laugh and they twirl,
With each silly sound, they're in a whirl.

So if you dive deep, keep your ears peeled wide,
For the giggles and snorts of the ocean's pride.
With each bubbling chuckle, the sea's full of cheer,
A symphony of laughter, for all who come near.

Lifting of the Marine Veil

Beneath the waves, where the currents are wild,
An octopus spins, looking charmingly styled.
In a top hat so grand, he throws a fine ball,
Inviting the fishes; come one, come all!

The seahorses prance, like they own the whole scene,
While sea cucumbers scoff, feeling quite mean.
"Who invited the crabs?" the clams all complain,
As they snap their tough shells in a regal disdain.

Snapping shrimp chatter, hoping to shine,
Sharing wild stories over oceanic wine.
Turtles in tuxedos, reserving a space,
With bubbles for cocktails, it's quite the cool pace.

As the flatfish roll in, wearing their shades,
The sea comes alive in its glorious parades.
Each creature so clever in the fun that they weave,
In this underwater feast, you'd never believe!

Foam-Kissed Breath of the Sea

With a puff and a blow, the surf starts to giggle,
Crabs play the banjo, as dolphins all wiggle.
The waves come crashing with pebbles and foam,
While seagulls above honk, and call it their home.

A starfish named Fred plays cards with the tide,
"Who'll bluff the great whales?" he asks with great pride.
The seaweed shakes hands, a fine deal to make,
As barnacles chuckle at this funny mistake.

The sun rays beam down, with laughter and light,
And the fish in their outfits dance all through the night.
A party of bubbles, each one is a friend,
And they spin in the splash till the fun has no end.

So dive in the surf and put worries on hold,
Join this wacky bash where the stories unfold.
For in every splash, there's a joke to be told,
In the foam-kissed waves, it's a sight to behold.

Cries of Old Giants

In the ocean's expanse, with a howl and a cheer,
The elders are groaning, but we're glad they are here.
With each mighty exhale, the tides swell with glee,
As the dolphins all laugh in splashing esprit.

Old fishes with tales of the years long gone by,
Swap stories of battles beneath the blue sky.
Jellyfish float by, with a soft glowing grin,
While the nail-biting shrimp run away with their kin.

"Remember the time that the Kraken came near?
What a ruckus that made and it's still crystal clear!"
With squishy sea stars rolling, a good time was had,
Over past pandemonium, folks are just glad.

So if you should wander into depths wild and free,
Look out for the giants who laugh with great glee.
Their cries are mere chuckles, of a life full of fun,
As they bask in the waves, together as one.

Ocean's Exhale

Bubbles rise like tiny spritz,
In the ocean, there's such a blitz.
Fish swim by in a hurry,
While crabs join in a flurry.

Seagulls dive for a snack, oh dear,
While dolphins weave without fear.
Splashing here, and splashing there,
Making waves, without a care.

In this vast blue, we find the jest,
Nature's laughter is truly the best.
With each puff and every splash,
Life in the sea is quite the bash.

Joyful, playful, a merry spree,
Under the sea, oh can't you see?
A party for creatures, big and small,
In the ocean, there's fun for all!

Serenade of the Deep

Hear the tune of seaweed sway,
An orchestra of fish at play.
Octopuses dance, quite a sight,
As starfish twirl in pure delight.

Shrimp perform a lively jig,
While a grouper dons a wig.
Krill provide a tiny beat,
As crabs tap-dance on their feet.

Anemones wave, like they're in cheer,
In this deep sea concert, all come near.
With bubbles popping, laughter rings,
The ocean sings of fun-filled things.

Together they form a lively band,
Making music across the sand.
In the depths, where antics thrive,
The serenade keeps joy alive!

Majesty of the Blue

Look at that whale, oh what a sight,
Waving its tail with all its might.
It splashes around, creates a scene,
Like a royal in a blue marine.

With a wink and a sly little play,
It flops on a wave, then swims away.
A mighty king, yet oh so spry,
In the ocean, it laughs and flies.

Sea turtles chuckle as they glide,
Sardines form a shimmering wide tide.
Together they giggle, part of the crew,
In this majesty that's funny and true.

As bubbles escape with a joyous sound,
The ocean holds laughter all around.
With each grand dive and playful spin,
The beauty of blue keeps the fun within!

Breath of the Tides

With each tide, comes a comical sway,
As sea cucumbers start their play.
They wiggle and giggle on the sand,
Making mischief, oh isn't it grand?

Jellyfish float like balloons in the air,
Making faces and causing a scare.
But with a grin, they drift and glide,
The ocean's charm, they cannot hide.

Crabs in a race, with a funny gait,
Do a sideways dance, oh isn't that great?
With starfish cheering from the rocks,
Under the sun, it's fun that knocks.

Echoes of laughter swirl and rise,
In this watery world where humor lies.
In the dance of the tides, fun sets sail,
Join the parade; we'll hear the tale!

Where the Great Ones Rest

In the ocean's big lounge chair,
Great ones lie without a care.
Puffing bubbles like a show,
Giggles echo from below.

With a splash and a snore,
They create seafoam galore.
Jellyfish dance on the floor,
While fish join in for encore.

Biggest jokes they like to tell,
As seabirds shout a loud 'Ahoy!'
Fins and flippers start to swell,
Tickling corals, oh what joy!

In this vast aquatic jest,
They find the ultimate rest.
Stars above join the fun too,
Wishing they could swim right through.

Timeless Calls of the Deep

Down below in liquid light,
Calls of the deep bring pure delight.
Echoes of laughter swirl and twine,
Water's giggles in rhythm align.

Crabs with caps do a little jig,
While seahorses pull their gig.
"Oh, I can't dance," the starfish sighs,
But wiggles happen, oh surprise!

Chasms of joy in every wave,
Making mischief, oh how they crave.
Bubble parties filled with cheer,
Everyone's welcome to come near.

Timeless calls rise like a tune,
Underneath the watchful moon.
With each chortle, sparkles gleam,
Creating a most watery dream.

The Glistening Whisper

A glistening whisper floats on high,
As dolphins leap and seagulls fly.
"Catch me if you can!" they tease,
With flips and spins that aim to please.

Crashing waves with jolly glee,
Echo laughter, wild and free.
Anemones wave in the cheer,
Pretending to be part of the steer.

Swirling currents make their play,
As narwhals join in the fray.
"Look at my horn!" they boast with pride,
In the silly ocean tide.

The glistening whisper, oh what a game,
Turning every fish into a name.
A party where all finned friends unite,
Underwater fun, a laughing sight!

A Ballet of the Brine

In a grand ocean stage so wide,
Creatures take their dance with pride.
Twirling krill, in casual flair,
While sardines form a sleek pair.

Clownfish chuckle, making a scene,
As octopuses follow their keen.
They sway to the rhythm of tides so bold,
In a ballet that never gets old.

Giant turtles, with grace and ease,
Do the twist with a gentle breeze.
With the currents, they glide and spin,
An underwater show that draws you in.

A ballet of bubbles, laughter, and fun,
Beneath the waves, under the sun.
So, swim along, don't just stand,
Join the dance in this grand sea band!

Tide's Sigh

In the ocean, things get silly,
A fish laughs, oh what a filly!
Bubbles burst like tiny balloons,
As crabs dance under the moon.

Seagulls squawk with such delight,
Splashing water's a messy fight.
A starfish spins, a dizzy sight,
While dolphins play, oh what a night!

A clam snaps shut, oh what a tease,
Tickled by a gentle breeze.
Seashells giggle on the shore,
As waves crash in, wanting more.

Laughter echoes through the tide,
An otter slides, oh what a ride!
With every wave, joy multiplies,
In this world where fun never dies.

Celestial Bubbles

Up above the sea so wide,
Stars flicker, like bubbles that glide.
Jellyfish float with lazy grace,
While fish wear smiles upon their face.

A whale sings a tune so sweet,
Making dolphins dance on their feet.
As crabs recite their silly limericks,
The ocean floor's full of antics.

With the tides, humor's our friend,
In laughter, we find no end.
Each surf's a cheer, every splash a joke,
A dance floor for all, beneath the oak.

So let the currents tickle your soul,
Join the sea critters in their rollicking goal.
Bubbles burst with giggles galore,
In this whimsical realm by the shore.

Vibration of the Deep Blue

Deep in the ocean's funny heart,
Seahorses strut, each playing a part.
Fish don tuxedos, ready to dance,
While the octopus gives a prancing glance.

Bubbles bounce, like little cheerleaders,
Waves dressed in foam, oh, what fun leaders!
Crabs wear hats that bob and sway,
Making silliness their daily play.

A starfish shows off its best moves,
While the turtles play groovy grooves.
Mermaids laugh, flipping their hair,
In this underwater circus fair.

With each splash, a joyous breach,
The deep blue's a wise, wacky beach.
So dive in deep, and don't be shy,
Join the giggles as the fish all fly!

Currents of Memory

In the swirl of the sea's embrace,
Every wave tells a funny face.
Fish reminisce, spinning their yarns,
About shipwrecks and old sea barns.

The gulls gossip from above,
While the barnacles hug with love.
A knitting turtle stitches a scarf,
Made of kelp, oh what a laugh!

Anemones wave, just like a hand,
Inviting joy from the sand.
Old stories dance through the tide,
As sea creatures take a silly ride.

So let the currents twist and whirl,
In this joyful, cackling swirl.
With every bubble, a memory's made,
In this oceanic escapade!

Breath of the Endless Deep

In the ocean, bubbles rise,
A fish jokes, oh what a surprise,
With each breath, the sea does laugh,
A splash, a wave, it's quite the gaffe.

The octopus waves, a cheeky grin,
While clam shells play a violin,
The shark tells tales of being cool,
As crabs dance off, splashing in the pool.

The seaweed sways, it's quite the sight,
Dancing to tunes of pure delight,
A dolphin flips, with grace and ease,
While a starfish laughs, teasing the breeze.

So next time you dip your toes,
Remember the jokes the ocean knows,
In every bubble, a giggle's caught,
In the deep blue world, laughter is sought.

Currents Whispering Through Time

In swirling tides, a whisper's found,
As fish swim 'round without a sound,
A sea turtle grins with a wink,
Saying, 'I'm older than you think!'

Anemones play hide and seek,
While jellyfish float, feeling chic,
A boat's squeak makes a crab take flight,
In this deep dance of sheer delight.

The currents swirl with stories galore,
Of nautical pranks from days of yore,
With barnacles sharing a hearty laugh,
And plankton composing their own epitaphs.

So when you gaze upon the sea,
Remember its humor, wild and free,
For in its depths, with bubbles and rhyme,
Every splash tells a joke, through time.

Harmonies Beneath the Waves

In oceans deep, a rumble glides,
Bubbles burst with silly strides.
A fish sings low, but off the beat,
While dolphins dance on flippered feet.

A gurgle here, a splashy show,
Seashells giggle, don't you know?
A crab does the twist, his friends all cheer,
While seaweed sways, it's party gear!

Octopus plays the deep-sea sax,
With pirate tunes, they all relax.
A turtle's slow, but groovy too,
As currents sway and laughter's due.

So join the fun, come take a dive,
Where under waves, the jesters thrive.
In this blue world of joy and cheer,
The ocean sings, let's all come near!

Dance of the Marine Titans

Beneath the waves, a giant sways,
With awkward moves in coral bays.
A kraken waltzes, arms amiss,
While fishes giggle, what a bliss!

A seal in shades, he flips with flair,
While jellyfish float without a care.
Anemones clap, getting in the groove,
The clumsy plankton can't help but move!

With every splash, a series of laughs,
As mermaids cheer for all the half-hearted drafts.
A whale tries breakdancing, oh what a sight,
As bubbles pop, and all feels right.

So come join in, don't stay up high,
Where dances are weird, but spirits fly.
In underwater ball, come find your fate,
Among the titans, don't be late!

Liquid Lullaby

In waters soft, where giggles dwell,
A narwhal hums a silly spell.
With bubbles popping like tiny drums,
Sardines sway, shaking their rumps.

A sleepy whale snores, but oh so loud,
Sending ripples to the next fish crowd.
A starfish claps, lost in the sound,
While sea turtles sway round and round.

Soft currents sing a lullaby sweet,
Sea creatures dream in their cozy seat.
A crab in pajamas, ready for bed,
With pillow of kelp beneath his head.

So if you dive into the moonlit sea,
Join the chorus, wild and free.
In liquid dreams, let laughter flow,
For under the waves, the jests do grow!

Whispers of the Ocean's Soul

In crystal depths, a secret giggle,
Coral reefs sway, with a happy wiggle.
A dolphin whispers jokes so bright,
As the tide draws near to the moonlight.

A seahorse spins, with a quirky flair,
While clams crack up, without a care.
The sea anemone shakes its head,
As turtles chuckle and find their bed.

With every wave, a joke unspools,
The jellyfish dance, breaking all the rules.
A fish in a tux, just for the night,
Makes the starfish laugh till morning light.

So hear the whispers where waters swirl,
Come join the chaos, give it a twirl.
For in the ocean's heart, so tender,
Lies joy and laughter, always to remember!

Breath of the Deep Ocean Spirit

In the deep where bubbles pop,
Fish gossip, and turtles stop.
A beluga with a big old grin,
Swaps jokes with a dolphin twin.

Octopus has eight arms to wave,
Telling tales of the brave and the knave.
Sea cucumbers roll their eyes,
While starfish spin their own surprise.

Scallops clap, a show of cheer,
While schools of fish swim near and dear.
Anemones dance in a wobbly trance,
Even crabs attempt to prance.

So in the dark, where laughter flows,
The ocean's spirit ever glows.
With a splash and a giggle, we sway,
In this watery world, come laugh and play!

Beneath the Moonlit Waves

Beneath the waves, where shadows creep,
Crabs tell tales before they sleep.
The moon above, it starts to glow,
While fish join in with a little show.

A sea lion juggling with fishy flair,
Turns the tide into a comedy fair.
Whales hum tunes, bass so divine,
As seahorses dance, trying to align.

The jellyfish glow in a silly parade,
Playing tag with the plans they made.
A clownfish shows off its best bright hue,
While plankton giggle at the spectacle too.

So come dive deep, where laughs intertwine,
In the ocean's glow, it's all so fine.
Under the moon, let your worries slip,
Join this party, don't miss the trip!

Oceanic Reverberations

In the pool of the blue, the sounds create,
Bubbles pop and giggles resonate.
A tuna breaks out in spontaneous dance,
While crabs click-clack in a sideways prance.

Echoes roll like waves at sea,
A friendly fish calls out, "Come play with me!"
Kelp sways to a beat only they know,
Whales raise their voices in a golden show.

Even in darkness, hear ballads ring,
As the flounder plays flute—the ocean's spring.
Clownfish sing, a chorus of fun,
Underwater theater, second to none.

Join the laughter, oh, don't be late,
In every splash, there's a chance to celebrate.
With the currents' hum as our guiding light,
Let's dance til dawn, the future feels bright!

Calling of the Sea Giants

Giant echoes ripple through the tide,
As the sea giants begin to glide.
With a splash and a splash, they give a cheer,
While barnacles giggle, "We love it here!"

Lofty tales of ocean past,
They swish and swirl, a dance so fast.
An orca wears a top hat, quite absurd,
While squid spin stories, in floating herds.

From the depths, a friendly roar,
The manta rays beckon from the ocean floor.
With a wink and a flip, they share a grin,
In this grand show, let the fun begin!

So come lend an ear to the mighty sea,
In their jovial realm, you'll find glee.
With each mighty breath, laughter springs,
In the calling of these ocean kings!

www.ingramcontent.com/pod-product-compliance
Lightning Source LLC
Chambersburg PA
CBHW070006300426
43661CB00141B/251